A Glut of Citrus Fruit

Ann Carr

Illustrated by
Martin MacKeown

MEREHURST PRESS
——— LONDON ———

*The Publishers wish to thank
Rosemary Wilkinson and Malcolm Saunders
for their help with this book.*

First published 1988 by Merehurst Press
5 Great James Street
London WC1N 3DA

Produced by
Malcolm Saunders Publishing Ltd
26 Ornan Road, London NW3 4QB

Copyright © 1988 this edition
Malcolm Saunders Publishing Ltd
Copyright © 1988 text Ann Carr
Copyright © 1988 design
and illustrations Martin MacKeown

ISBN 0 948075 85 6

Photoset in Linotype Ehrhardt
by Fakenham Photosetting Limited
Printed in Spain

CONTENTS

FOREWORD

Whatever the season, whether in sizzling heat or crisp frost, citrus fruit piled high in shops and markets are a wonderful sight, with their clean, sharp colours. They may be set among far rarer, more exotic beauties but they hold their own special place with their seemingly limitless uses, from medicinal to the more obvious culinary.

Tisanes and tinctures often contain their juices and oils; the peels can be dried and added to a pot-pourri together with orris root, rose petals, lavender, spices and other flower petals and halved grapefruit shells are a well-known slug trap in the garden.

Unless your garden is in a Mediterranean-type climate, California, Florida or in the southern hemisphere, the gluts will be found in shops and markets, where boxes of imported Seville oranges or trays of satsumas are available at remarkably low prices. Don't be afraid of the citrus glut: use it to experiment with. Make a marinade of orange or grapefruit juice with a little oil and some herbs and turn a joint of pork in it for 2 to 3 days. Drink lots of freshly squeezed orange juice for breakfast and feel healthy: it's not an extravagance, oranges are full of vitamin C. A little grapefruit will sharpen a too-sweet dish of carrots and lemon will cut the fat in a rich pork casserole. Limes are good in sorbets, mousses and creams.

Citrus fruit, of all the fruit available to us, are the most diverse in their uses.

In the eighteenth of Edward the first (1290) a large Spanish ship came into Portsmouth; out of the cargo of which the Queen bought fifteen citrons and seven oranges.

> *(1841, Roxburghe Club, Manners and household expenses of England in the thirteenth and fifteenth centuries)*

10

INTRODUCTION

If you walk through a grove of ripe orange or lemon trees at dusk, you will see the fruits glowing like lanterns amongst the dark green leaves; an experience surpassed only by walking through the same groves at blossom time when the scent is unbelievably powerful and heady.

In the past it was common for the great houses in northern Europe to be built with an orangery; an elegant south-facing garden house with a long wall of glass doors, which could be opened wide to let in sun and air. Here the owners could stroll on fine sunny days delighting in the glory of their orange trees in blossom or in the fruit which held much-needed vitamins through the long, lean, northern winters.

Modern storage and transport have made citrus fruit available to us all the year round and, through constant experimentation, new strains of fruit trees are being developed with ever-longer fruiting seasons. Thus, not only do we have regular supplies of citrus fruit but also they are fresher and in better condition than previously, because they have not been subjected to over-long storage.

If you have access to fruit from the tree, pick when just ripe: the fruit will store without harm for three to four months in a cool, dry place. However, there is nothing more wonderful to use in cooking than the fruit straight from the trees.

Oranges belong to the genus *citrus*, of the family *rutaceae*, to which the shrub herb, rue, also belongs. The word 'orange' derives from the Arabic 'nāranj', for the Arabs, it is thought, were the first to bring the orange from the Orient and introduced it to Europe by planting in their Spanish colony, probably its bitter form, the Seville orange. It has been suggested that the orange missed the usual trade route through Asia Minor and came instead by Arab dhow from India to the Red Sea coast of Egypt. From there it

was most likely transported by camel to the Nile, thence by Nile boat to Alexandria and then by ship across the Mediterranean to Ostia, the port of Rome. Now oranges are a well-established Mediterranean fruit crop.

They are cultivated commercially in subtropical and tropical America, northern and eastern Mediterranean countries, Australia and South Africa.

Before 1920 the orange was used mainly as a dessert fruit; the popularity of orange juice in the 1930s changed that.

If you are lucky enough to live where you can grow your own oranges, the *Encyclopaedia Britannica* suggests that the trees thrive in a wide range of soils and can even withstand the occasional light frost.

The lemon tree, 'citrus limon', also belongs to the family *rutaceae*, though it is smaller than the orange. This beautiful tree with its scented flowers and mystical fruit has been cultivated in Europe since the first century A.D. It came from the East, although its exact origin is not known – the Indus valley being the most convincing suggestion.

Today lemons are grown principally on or near the Mediterranean coast. Sicily is one of the main producers; probably the Moors brought the lemon there at the same time as they introduced the fruit to Spain. It is also grown in America, particularly in California and Arizona. Florida is both too wet and too cold for this evergreen tree, which, although it requires less total heat throughout the year than the orange, dislikes frost, heavy rain and too much hot sun.

Lemon trees do not breed 'true' from seed and are, therefore, usually propagated by budding the desired variety on to the rootstocks of other citrus fruit; bitter orange, tangerine and grapefruit often being used.

Limes, *citrus aurantifolia*, small, pale green echoes of the lemon, seem to be rather sourer but their culinary uses are much the same. They are also very popular for use in drinks and cordials.

Limes are grown in the U.S.A. and throughout the West Indies and South America. The fruit is full of juice and has a

high vitamin C content. There are several varieties of lime: the West Indian lime, the Persian lime (grown in Florida), the Indian and the Tahiti lime; all differ in shape, size, colour, acidity and flavour. The most noticeably different is the Indian lime, which is small and rather more yellow than green in colour. Sweet limes are now not much grown and anyway are sadly insipid in flavour.

In Europe the lime is still rarer than the lemon, so that there is unlikely to be a great surplus of them in the markets.

The grapefruit is not a hybrid, nor the result of years of careful plant breeding but a new species, not yet 200 years old – a mere baby compared to other citrus fruit. Its birthplace was Jamaica and the introduction to that island of the pomelo seems to have been crucial.

Something seems to have happened to the pomelo after it was brought by Captain Shaddock to Jamaica from south-east Asia. Some botanists think that a natural cross occurred in the wild between it and the citron (see below), resulting in the grapefruit; others think that the pomelo, by mutation, produced the grapefruit all by itself!

Our name 'grapefruit' derives from the fact that the fruit hangs from the tree in clusters, grapelike. The Dutch, French and German words for the grapefruit are 'pompelmoes', 'pamplemousse' and 'pampelmuse' – all derived, one imagines, from the Dutch East Indies pomelo. The pomelo itself was first recorded on the Chinese mainland as early as 1500 B.C.

The main growing area in the world for the grapefruit is now the United States: California, Florida, Texas and Arizona. They are also grown round the Mediterranean but their quality is inferior. The grapefruit is hardier than the lemon and, like the orange, can survive a touch of frost.

There are now many varieties of grapefruit available: thick-skinned, thin-skinned, seedless and, of course, the pink grapefruit. On the whole the sweetest and juiciest are the thin-skinned.

Apart from locally-grown gluts, grapefruit are widely available all year round, although

Clementine

shops and markets themselves create gluts by
bulk-buying, so that it is possible several
times a year to buy the fruit at a bargain price.

The same cannot be said of the other citrus fruit in this group: pomelo, ugli and citron. The first two are available seasonally
and it is interesting to compare them with the
grapefruit. The citron, *citrus medica*, is a large
lemon-like fruit but with a rougher, thicker
skin. The fresh fruit is available for a short
season in Israel, immediately after Yom Kip-
pur and a sweet variety is grown in Corsica. It
is rarely obtainable fresh in the U.K., though
the candied fruit is available all year round. It
is the best of the candied peels with a sharp
freshness. In France a citron paste is made,
pâte de céderat, and the lemon-tasting liqueur
of Greece is, in fact, citron-flavoured.
Although this fruit is so seldom seen fresh in
European shops and markets it is thought to
have been the first citrus fruit to have
reached Europe.

Mandarin, tangerine, satsuma and
clementine, *citrus reticulata*, are all known as

loose-skinned oranges. Though this is not strictly true of the thin-skinned, heavenly-sweet and scented clementine, it is so of the other three fruit whose skins do not cling to their flesh. These fruits are usually available in Europe only during the winter months and they have come to be associated with Christmas. In some European countries they are traditionally used to decorate the Christmas tree.

Tangelo and minneola are both crosses between tangerines and grapefruit. It is unlikely that there will be a glut of these fruits on the market but there may be trays of tangerines and satsumas available at bargain prices towards the end of the season.

The kumquat (meaning 'golden orange' in Cantonese) is not included in the recipes in this book as it is not widely available. It is interesting to note, however, that there is some doubt as to whether or not it actually belongs to the citrus family. Until recently it has not been known much outside its native China; now, however, it is grown commercially in the United States.

Satsuma

Approximate Measures of Fruit Juice & Peel

1 orange produces 2–3 fl oz (60–90 ml) juice

3 oranges produce 8–10 fl oz (250–315 ml) juice

1 lemon produces 1½–2 fl oz (40–60 ml) juice

1 lime produces 1–1½ fl oz (30–40 ml) juice

1 grapefruit produces 5–6 fl oz (155–185 ml) juice

1 mandarin or loose-skinned fruit produces 2–3 fl oz (60–90 ml) juice

Grated Peel

1 orange produces 3 teaspoons peel

1 lemon produces 2–3 teaspoons peel

1 lime produces 1–2 teaspoons peel

1 grapefruit produces 3–4 teaspoons peel

1 mandarin or loose-skinned fruit produces 1–2 teaspoons peel

Olive Oil

Where this is specified in the ingredients, do try to use it, choosing a good quality olive oil if possible. It is not extravagant; olive oil and citrus fruit seem to have a natural affinity.

COOKS' NOTES

1. Unless specific details are given in the individual recipes, the following apply:

– spoon measurements are level

– sugar is granulated

– eggs are standard size

2. Follow either the imperial measurements or the metric but do not mix them, as they have been calculated separately.

3. As individual oven temperatures vary, use the timings in the recipes as a guide. Always preheat your oven or grill.

The
Recipes

LEMONS

The lemon is the most versatile of ingredients in the kitchen. This beautiful fruit can be dried or pickled, grated, sliced or squeezed. The oil from the thinly-pared peel of a very fresh lemon will subtly flavour hot milk or cream and a slice of lemon in a glass of cold water is wonderfully refreshing on a hot day – these are just two very simple examples of dramatic changes which the use of lemon can bring about to the most basic of ingredients.

Lemons can also be used to flavour sauces and syrups, cakes and confectionery and to enhance and sharpen bland fruit and vegetables, fish or meat. Like vinegar they can be used as a tenderizer or as a short-term preservative, and, also like vinegar, they can be added to olive oil to make a salad dressing or marinade. Indeed, in Turkey, Greece and North Africa the lemon is used for these purposes almost as much as vinegar. The lemon is more widely used in the kitchen than any other citrus fruit but, unlike them, it is never eaten whole, although it can be pickled or dried whole.

Limes can be substituted for lemons in many recipes. Though slightly smaller than lemons, they contain a lot of juice. They are thinner-skinned than lemons and therefore dry out quickly. They are especially good with fish or in cold soufflés and creams.

Chicken Stock

The peel and juice of citrus fruits vastly improve and lighten a stock. This stock can be used as a basis for soups or sauces; clarified, it makes a nourishing broth to which you can add vegetables, pasta, rice or eggs. It is easy to make and can be frozen in small or large quantities.

Flavour the stock with either lemon or orange: never both. If you make a stock of game bones at Christmas, flavour this with tangerines, mandarins or any loose-skinned citrus fruit peel, together with the juice if possible. Old boiling birds are cheap and lean and so do not produce a fatty stock. Use the shells of either lemons or oranges after the juice has been extracted for some other purpose.

1 whole chicken, cut into pieces
½ onion
4 carrots, scraped
1 stick celery, leaves included
peel of 1 lemon i.e. 2 lemon shells or peel of 2 oranges (4 orange halves)
8 black peppercorns
80 fl oz (2.5 litres) cold water

Trim off all fatty bits and wash chicken pieces. Place in a deep saucepan, add all other ingredients, cover and simmer for 2 to

3 hours over a low heat, skimming off any scum.

Strain liquid into a large bowl and leave overnight to cool thoroughly. Next day, skim off all fat and return liquid to a clean saucepan. Bring to the boil and continue to boil for 3 minutes, then pour into clean containers and store in the fridge.

To clarify the soup: add 2 to 3 lightly beaten egg whites and the egg shells to every 2 pints (1.25 litres) of the strained and skimmed stock. Bring to the boil, then strain through a piece of muslin.

Note: if the stock is to be kept for longer than 2 to 3 days, it is wiser to freeze it as soon as it is cold.

I will be with you in the squeezing of a Lemon.
(1773, Oliver Goldsmith 'She Stoops to
Conquer')

Quick & Simple Lemon Soup

Good hot or cold. To serve 6, heat 40 fl oz (1.25 litres) chicken stock in a pan together with a little grated nutmeg, the peel and juice of 1 lemon, salt and freshly ground black pepper, to taste. Just before serving, add 6 fl oz (185 ml) double (heavy) cream and 1 tablespoon chopped fresh parsley. Pour into a warmed serving bowl.

If serving cold, stir the cream into the soup after it has cooled, then chill. Sprinkle with parsley just as the soup is ready for the table.

Note: if using a lemon-flavoured stock, you may like to use only half the quantities of lemon suggested above.

The scurvy has hardly been known in our navy since limes and lemons were ordered by law to be carried by all vessels sailing to foreign parts.
(John Yeats 'Natural History of Commerce')

I drank water and limmons, by Phisitions advise.
(1594, A letter of Lady Russell, from Sir Henry
Ellis's 'Original letters illustrative of English
History')

Lemon & Beetroot Soup

Quick to make, this soup is good hot or cold
and looks appetizing and pretty. If serving
hot, accompany with triangles of brown
bread and butter; if cold, with lemon slices.

Serves 6
3 medium-sized cooked beetroot
$^{1}/_{2}$ small onion, finely chopped
30 fl oz (940 ml) vegetable stock
2 teaspoons grated lemon peel
juice of 2 lemons
$^{1}/_{4}$ teaspoon grated nutmeg
1–2 oz (30–60 g) sugar, or to taste
salt and pepper, to taste

TO FINISH
10 fl oz (315 ml) plain yogurt and 6 fl oz
(185 ml) double (heavy) cream or 14 fl oz
(440 ml) sour cream
brown bread and butter or lemon slices, to
serve

Peel and chop beetroot, place in a blender or
food processor with onion and process to a

fine purée, slowly adding half the stock. Pour into a saucepan, add remaining stock, lemon peel, lemon juice, spice, sugar, salt and pepper. Bring to the boil, cover and simmer gently for 8 to 10 minutes. Meanwhile, beat together yogurt and cream, if using.

To serve hot, pour into a warmed soup tureen, add half the yogurt and cream or the sour cream, stir once and ladle into individual soup bowls. Hand round remaining cream separately, together with bread and butter.

If serving cold, stir half the cream mixture into cold soup, ladle into bowls or soup plates and float a slice of lemon on top. Hand round the extra yogurt and cream or sour cream.

Lemon & Artichoke Salad

This salad uses the root vegetable, the Jerusalem artichoke. It makes a wonderful starter when used in this way. Choose large artichokes if possible.

Serves 6

1–1½ lb (500–750 g) Jerusalem artichokes, depending on size

salt

juice of 2 lemons plus 2 tablespoons lemon juice

grated peel of 1 lemon

3 spring onions, green and white parts chopped

2 fl oz (60 ml) olive oil

freshly ground black pepper, to taste

6 fl oz (185 ml) single (light) cream

2 tablespoons chopped fresh parsley

Scrape artichokes and remove some of the smallest, most awkward knobs and knobbles. Boil in salted water, to which you have

The Citron perfumes the air for many miles round the city.
(Washington Irving 'The Lives of Mahomet and his Successors')

added 2 tablespoons lemon juice, for 10 to 20 minutes, depending on size; they should be firm and whole, not mushy when cooked. Remove with a slotted spoon, as they are done and leave to cool. Then, while still just warm, slice, cube or quarter; place in a serving dish, add remaining lemon juice, lemon peel, spring onions and olive oil, toss very gently, taking care not to break the artichokes and leave to marinate for 1 to 2 hours. Just before serving, grind over some black pepper, pour over cream, toss again and sprinkle with parsley.

Lemon & Fish Starter

The lemon in this recipe balances the slight oiliness of the mackerel. This dish needs good quality olive oil.

Serves 4

2 fl oz (60 ml) olive oil

4 small mackerel, cleaned, washed and dried

4 cloves garlic, chopped

salt, to taste

juice of 3 lemons

plenty of freshly ground black pepper

2 tablespoons chopped fresh parsley

TO FINISH

1 lemon, cut in wedges

12 or more black olives

Heat oil in a heavy frying pan over a low heat, add fish and garlic and cook gently, turning once or twice, for 10 to 12 minutes, or until fish is cooked through. Sprinkle with salt, add lemon juice, turn fish and transfer to a deep serving platter. Pour over pan juices and garlic, then leave to cool. To serve, grind pepper over fish, sprinkle with parsley and garnish with lemon wedges and olives.

The Lemon and the piercing Lime
Their lighter glories blend.
> *(1727, James Thomson 'The Seasons (summer)')*

Pot Roast of Chicken with Lemon

Most dishes using lemon are improved by the use of olive oil. This is particularly good served with a dish of pasta tossed in butter and parsley.

Serves 4
2 fl oz (60 ml) olive oil
1 × 3½ lb (1.75 kg) roasting chicken, dressed
3 lemons, sliced
8 cloves garlic, peeled
4 sprigs fresh thyme
8 fl oz (250 ml) white stock
salt and pepper, to taste

Heat oil in a casserole with a tight-fitting lid, add chicken, lemon slices and garlic cloves. Gently fry for 8 to 10 minutes, turning chicken over and over, then add sprigs of thyme, stock, salt and pepper, cover tightly and pot roast for 1 hour, or until chicken is cooked through.

Chicken in a Basket

This dish, as eaten in pubs where it has been first frozen then deep-fried in poor fat, is a travesty of the real thing, for which the recipe is quick, simple and unbelievably good.

Use chicken quarters from a small tender roasting bird, preferably free range and corn fed. For each chicken piece allow ½–1 oz (15–30 g) butter, 1–2 fl oz (30–60 ml) lemon juice and plenty of freshly ground black pepper. Preheat the grill. Melt the butter in a frying pan, add the lemon juice and pepper and toss the chicken pieces in this mixture, then place under the hot grill and grill for 5 to 6 minutes on each side, basting frequently with the lemon and butter mixture. Don't worry if the chicken pieces scorch a bit: they are meant to.

When they are cooked through, serve at once, accompanied by the pan juices, plenty of fresh bread and a tossed green salad.

Poungarnets, Lemmanz, and Pipinz.
(Robert Laneham 'A letter whearin, part of the
entertainment untoo the Queenz Maiesty, at
Killingworth Castl is signified')

Russian Lemon Cheesecake

This cheesecake is rather solid but none the less delicious. Try it for lunch with a fresh orange salad dusted with sugar and cinnamon.

Serves 8
1 lb (500 g) curd cheese
2 oz (60 g) butter, melted
2 oz (60 g) semolina
3 oz (90 g) sugar
1 egg yolk
1 whole egg
grated peel and juice of 1 lemon
1 teaspoon vanilla extract
2 oz (60 g) candied mixed peel
1 tablespoon crushed biscuit crumbs
sour cream, to serve, if desired

Beat curd cheese together with melted butter in a blender or food processor. Add semolina, sugar, egg yolk, whole egg, lemon peel and juice and vanilla extract and process again briefly to mix. Fold in the candied peel. Lavishly butter an 8 in (20 cm) cake tin with a removable base and coat well with crumbs. Pour curd cheese mixture into the tin and bake at 180 °C (350 °F/Gas 4) for 40 to 50 minutes or until firm in the middle when cake tin is gently shaken. Eat hot or cold with sour cream if liked.

Lemon & Currant Cake

Serves 6–8
4 oz (125 g) butter
4 oz (125 g) sugar
2 eggs
grated peel of 2 lemons
2 oz (60 g) candied peel, preferably lemon
but mixed will do
2 oz (60 g) currants
4 oz (125 g) ground almonds
4 oz (125 g) self-raising flour

Beat butter and sugar together in a bowl or a food processor until light and fluffy, then add eggs one by one, beating well in between. Stir in lemon peel, candied peel, currants and almonds and lastly fold in flour. Pour into a buttered and floured 8 in (20 cm) cake tin and bake at 180 °C (350 °F/Gas 4) for 30 to 40 minutes or until a skewer inserted into the middle comes out clean.

A Filling for a Lemon Tart

This delicious mixture, half marmalade and half curd comes from 'The Book of Domestic Cookery', published in 1829. I have adapted it for the modern cook.

4 lemons
4 oz (125 g) ground almonds
8 oz (250 g) sugar
2 eggs, beaten
1 1/2 oz (40 g) butter

Pare peel from lemons, place in a saucepan, cover with water and bring to the boil. Drain, cover with fresh water and boil until very tender, checking regularly to ensure water doesn't boil dry: it will take 30 to 40 minutes. Remove and chop very, very finely, until peel looks like breadcrumbs. Squeeze lemon juice and place in a saucepan with chopped peel, almonds, beaten egg and sugar. Stir over a low heat until the mixture thickens. Stir in butter. Cool and use to fill a large tart or tartlets.

Lemon & Egg Jelly

An old-fashioned pudding that used to be called 'lemon solid'. It is quite unlike its old name and is neither a jelly nor a blancmange but rather a combination of the two and nicer than either.

Serves 6
½ oz (15 g) powdered gelatine
20 fl oz (625 ml) water
grated peel and juice of 2 lemons
3 oz (90 g) sugar
4 eggs
10 fl oz (315 ml) double (heavy) cream
2 tablespoons rum
1 teaspoon caster sugar

Heat together gelatine, water and lemon peel in a saucepan. Stir until all the gelatine is dissolved but do not allow to boil. Strain and reserve. Beat sugar and eggs together in a bowl using a wooden spoon, pour on the hot liquid and return to the pan. Cook gently as for a custard, again, do not allow to boil and stir constantly until the mixture thickens slightly, then add lemon juice, reheat gently and strain into a wetted jelly mould or a pretty glass dish. Cool, then place in the fridge until set.

To serve, whip cream with rum and caster sugar, turn out the mould and smother with flavoured cream.

Lemon Creams

This is a lovely old-fashioned recipe, both rich and fresh tasting. It is also very simple to make.

Serves 6
1 lemon
20 fl oz (625 ml) cream
4 egg yolks
4 oz (125 g) caster sugar
sponge fingers, to serve

Thinly pare peel from lemon and infuse with cream by gently heating the two together in a heavy saucepan and leaving over a low heat for about 10 minutes. Meanwhile, place egg yolks and sugar in a bowl and, using a wooden spoon, cream together until almost no grittiness remains and the mixture is ribbon-like when poured off the spoon. Bring cream and peel to the boil and pour over egg yolk mixture. Return to the pan and cook very gently over a low heat until the mixture coats the back of the spoon. Squeeze juice from lemon. When cream is almost cold, stir in lemon juice. Serve in small cups, pots or old-fashioned custard glasses with sponge fingers.

A little Greeke Barke loaded with tunnes of Lemon Juyce which the Turks drink like Nectar.
(1617, Fynes Moryson 'An Itinerary')

The Ile enricht us with many good things; Orenges, Lemons, Lymes.

(1638, Sir Thomas Herbert)

Lemon Biscuits

4 oz (125 g) butter, cut into small pieces
8 oz (250 g) plain flour
4 oz (125 g) caster sugar
4 teaspoons grated lemon peel
1/4–1/2 teaspoon ground mace, or to taste
1 egg yolk
1–2 tablespoons lemon juice

In a large mixing bowl (or a food processor) rub fat into flour until it looks like fine bread-crumbs. Add caster sugar, lemon peel and mace and mix well together. Beat egg yolk and half the lemon juice together, reserving remainder in case dough is too stiff. Pour egg mixture onto flour and press together until the dough sticks together but is not too soft or too crumbly to roll out. Add reserved lemon juice as necessary if too stiff. Turn onto a floured board, divide into two and roll out to about 1/8 in (0.3 cm) thick, cut into rounds with a pastry cutter. Place on a buttered baking tray and bake at 180°C (350°F/Gas 4) for 10 to 15 minutes, until crisp and lightly coloured.

To Pickle Lemons

This recipe also comes from 'The Book of Domestic Cookery', 1829. I give it in its original version and afterwards my own adaptation for you to try.

Lemon Ketchup or Pickle

'Cut 3 large juicy lemons across the top and stuff salt into them; set them upright in a dish before the fire and turn them every day. When they become dry roast them in a Dutch oven until they become brown. Boil a quart of vinegar, with a quarter of a pound of anchovies, without the bones and scales (but do not wash them), four blades of mace, half a nutmeg sliced, and a spoonful of white pepper; boil gently ten minutes; then pour it, boiling hot, on the lemons, in a stone jar; and cover close. Let it stand six weeks, then put it into quarter-pint flat bottles. It is excellent for made dishes and the lemon eats well.'

Lemon Pickle

Use in casseroles or stews or serve with cold meats.

3 lemons
salt
4 blades mace
1/2 crushed nutmeg
10 whole allspice
24 black peppercorns
40 fl oz (1.25 litres) wine vinegar
1 lb (500 g) brown sugar

Cut tops off lemons, sprinkle well with salt, pressing it in and stand upright on a wire rack on a tray in a warm, dry place (the airing cupboard or a radiator will do very well). They won't need turning and will take 2 to 4 weeks to dry out, depending on the heat source. Once dry, finish off in the oven. They will colour slightly. Tie spices in a muslin bag and boil gently with vinegar for 15 to 20 minutes. Remove spice bag and pour vinegar over lemons and leave for 6 weeks. Using a slotted spoon, remove lemons and slice. Heat vinegar in a saucepan, add sugar and stir until dissolved, then boil for 5 minutes, pack lemon slices into clean jars, pour over vinegar syrup, cool and cover.

We wanted not for lemonade and other refreshing waters.

(1697, Countess d'Aunoy's Travels)

To Dry Whole Lemons or Limes

Take firm fresh lemons or limes and leave on a wire rack on a radiator. The lemons will turn dark and very slowly dry out, leaving a scented husk, which can be used in casseroles or stews. Alternatively, leave a whole lemon or shreds of lemon or orange peel to dry out in a dish of pot-pourri.

Lemonade

This is an unusual and refreshing beverage to make before Christmas if you can find Seville oranges. Children and adults love it.

Grate the peel of 1 lemon and 2 Seville oranges into a large bowl, squeeze the fruit and add the juice, then pour over 20 fl oz (625 ml) boiling water and stir in 4 oz (125 g) sugar, or more if you like. Cool and bottle. Keeps in the fridge for 2 to 3 weeks. Dilute with sparkling mineral water for a super refreshing pick-you-up on New Year's Day!

With lemonade he gargles first his throat.
(1791, William Gifford 'The Baviad')

Lime Icebox Cake

Served in slices with a fresh raspberry sauce, this is the prettiest of summer desserts.

Serves 8–10

SPONGE
2 eggs
2 tablespoons caster sugar
2 rounded tablespoons plain flour, sifted

FILLING
4 limes
2 egg whites
6 oz (185 g) sugar
16 fl oz (500 ml) double (heavy) cream

Butter two 8 in (20 cm) sandwich tins and dust with flour. Place eggs and sugar in a mixing bowl and whisk until pale and thick-

ened. Carefully fold in sifted flour, then divide mixture between two prepared tins. Bake at 190 °C (375 °F/Gas 5) for 15 minutes, until golden brown and springy to the touch. Turn out onto a wire rack and leave until cold, then cut sponge cakes into thin pieces and use to line sides and base of a 1½ lb (750 g) loaf tin or rectangular plastic freezer container.

Grate peel from all 4 limes (limes yield less peel than lemons) and squeeze the juice. Reserve both. Beat egg whites very, very stiffly, then gradually beat in 4 oz (125 g) of the sugar. Beat cream with remaining sugar, then carefully fold lime juice and peel into cream, do not beat at all, otherwise the mixture will become too stiff to handle. Fold in egg whites, pour into the lined tin, cover and freeze until firm, 3 to 4 hours.

Home-Made Candied Peel

Bought candied peel is usually so full of additives and preservative that it is worth making your own. Not only is it additive-free but it is fresh and has a wonderful tang, quite unlike the chewy bright pieces that are sold expensively in cartons.

8 oz (250 g) peel, orange, lemon or grapefruit, see method
8 oz (250 g) sugar
10–15 fl oz (315–470 ml) water

Using a sharp knife, mark peel in quarters from top to bottom of fruit and carefully

48

remove. Scrape or trim off as much white pith as possible. (Reserve the flesh for one of the other recipes.) Place peel in a bowl, cover with cold water and leave overnight.

Next day drain peel and place in a saucepan, pour over 10 fl oz (315 ml) water and bring to the boil. Add sugar, stir until dissolved, then remove from heat and leave overnight.

The following day, bring peel and syrup to the boil again, remove from heat and leave overnight once more.

On the final day, bring to the boil and simmer for 20 to 30 minutes or longer until the syrup forms a firm, soft ball when dropped into a cup of cold water. Remove from the heat and, using a slotted spoon, take out the peel and place on wire cooling racks. Leave to drain and cool, then dry off in the airing cupboard or other warm, dry place. Store in screw-topped jars in the piece. Cut only as needed.

Never without Limon-Peel in her Mouth, to correct an unsavoury Vapour of her Own.
(1694, Sir Roger L'Estrange 'The Fables of Aesop and other eminent mythologists, with morals and reflexions')

Lime Granita

Serves 6
4 oz (125 g) caster sugar
20 fl oz (625 ml) water
4 limes, peel grated and juice extracted
fresh lime slices, to decorate

Dissolve caster sugar in water in a heavy-bottomed saucepan over a low heat. Bring to the boil, then boil for 5 to 7 minutes. Remove from heat, then stir in grated peel and lime juice. Leave to infuse until cool, then strain into a freezing container. Cover and freeze for 2 hours or until the mixture is turning to ice crystals. Remove and mix, freeze for a further two hours, mix again and freeze until firm.

Before serving, remove from freezer and leave at room temperature for 10 minutes, mix and serve at once, decorated with slices of fresh lime.

ORANGES

The sour Seville orange may have been the first to be introduced to our kitchens but it is now generally only used during its short season for marmalade making, though grated or finely pared Seville orange peel will add a wonderful flavour to casseroles or creamy desserts.

It is the sweet orange that is now used in our cooking. This fruit, which we take so much for granted, imparts a marvellous flavour to stocks, soups, casseroles, cakes, ice creams, desserts and even fish dishes. What makes it particularly satisfying is that the whole fruit – peel, juice and flesh – can be used in one dish.

Tangerines, mandarins and clementines are all good in savoury and fruit salads, make good sorbets and, when added to a stock, will give a gentler flavour than the orange.

Kumquats are generally too tart to eat fresh. They are best cooked in a light syrup or preserved in a mixture of sugar syrup and alcohol.

Beef Stock

This, like chicken stock, is well worth making and freezing. It is useful for soups, sauces and gravies or clarified as a broth to which you can add finely diced vegetables, pasta or eggs.

2 lb (1 kg) lean beef
1 marrow bone
1 veal knuckle bone, cow heel or pig's trotter
120 fl oz (3.75 litres) water
1 fl oz (30 ml) oil, for frying
2 onions, chopped
4 carrots, scraped and chopped
4 sticks celery, chopped
2 oranges, stuck with 4 cloves
2 bay leaves
3 sprigs fresh thyme

Place meat and bones in a large, lidded saucepan, add water, bring to the boil, cover and simmer for 2 hours. Lift lid occasionally and remove any scum that may have formed on the surface.

Heat oil in a heavy-bottomed frying pan, add vegetables and stir-fry for 6 to 10 minutes. Remove from the heat, pour on a teacupful of hot stock, bring to the boil, then tip the contents of the frying pan into the stock. Add oranges, bay leaves and thyme, cover and simmer for a further 2 to 3 hours. The liquid should have reduced by a quarter to a third. Cool and strain. This should make a wonderful jelly-like stock. Clarify if you want to make a clear broth, see page 25, before adding salt and pepper and garnishes.

Navel

Orange & Raspberry Soup

A very pretty, simple summer soup.

Serves 4–5
1 lb (500 g) fresh raspberries
4 oz (125 g) sugar
20 fl oz (625 ml) fresh orange juice
10 fl oz (315 ml) sparkling mineral or
soda water
2 teaspoons chopped fresh mint
2–3 fl oz (60–90 ml) sour cream, to
finish

Purée raspberries with sugar in a blender or food processor, pour into a large bowl, then stir in orange juice and chill. Just before serving, add sparkling water and mint. Pour into bowls and decorate with a swirl of sour cream.

Orange & Spinach Salad

Serve as a side salad or starter. Take fresh young spinach leaves, wash well, dry and tear the leaves into manageable-sized pieces, removing any tough stalks. To every good handful of spinach, use 1 to 1½ oranges. Peel the oranges, remove all pith and slice. Toss well with a dressing of 3 parts olive oil and 1 part orange juice, to which you have added salt and pepper to taste and a little crushed garlic or, for a more delicate flavour, 1 tablespoon chopped chives.

This salad makes an unusual starter if you add warm, crispy bacon pieces to it after it has been tossed. Serve straightaway.

Maroc

Orange with Vegetables

Turnips, carrots, parsnips, swedes and potatoes all benefit from the addition of a little orange. Add peel to the steamer or cooking water, finish off carrots in a pan with butter, orange juice and a teaspoon of sugar. Turnips and parsnips can be finished with the same glaze. A purée of potatoes is much improved by the addition of 2–4 fl oz (60–125 ml) orange juice, ½ a teaspoon of grated peel and a pinch of ground mace or ground ginger, all beaten in with a good nut of butter.

Salad vegetables, too, are enhanced by marinating in orange juice, especially tomatoes, sliced and the juice poured over, and cucumber treated in the same way. Sprinkle with chives, salt and pepper and serve.

Carrots with Orange

A delicately-flavoured summer dish for young carrots.

Serves 4

1½ lb (750 g) finger-sized carrots, scraped

6 fl oz (185 ml) orange juice

salt and pepper, to taste

1 oz (30 g) butter

2 teaspoons chopped fresh marjoram leaves

Place carrots and orange juice in a pan. Add salt, cover and cook for 7 to 10 minutes, until cooked but still crisp. Shake the pan occasionally to ensure all carrots are cooked evenly. Drain, add butter, marjoram and pepper, toss and serve.

Reserve juice for a sauce or summer soup.

Rice, Orange & Grapefruit Salad

A colourful, fresh-tasting summer dish.

Serves 4

2 cups cooked long-grain rice, still warm

6 tablespoons olive oil

1 tablespoon wine vinegar

1 teaspoon Dijon mustard

1 orange, peeled and chopped

1 grapefruit, peeled and chopped

2 tablespoons black olives, stoned and halved

1 tablespoon chopped spring onions

2 tablespoons chopped fresh parsley

salt and pepper, to taste

Place warm rice in a bowl. Mix oil, vinegar and mustard together in a screw-topped jar, shake well, then pour over rice and leave to cool. Just before serving, mix in all the other ingredients. Taste and adjust seasoning as necessary.

The rinde of the Orrendge is hot, and the meate within it is cold.

(1587, Arthur Golding 'P. de Mornay's Woorke concerning the trewness of the Christian religion')

Fish with Orange, Apple & Horseradish Sauce

An unusual combination of flavours. Served with a salad of orange and watercress and with plain, boiled potatoes it is excellent. Grated horseradish can be bought in jars.

Serves 4–5

2 fl oz (60 ml) olive oil or 1 1/2 oz (40 g) butter

2 lb (1 kg) cod, haddock or halibut fillets

2 eating apples

juice of 2 oranges

1–2 teaspoons sugar, or to taste

1 teaspoon vinegar

1 tablespoon fresh grated horseradish

3–4 fl oz (90–125 ml) double (heavy) cream

salt and pepper, to taste

slices of orange and parsley sprigs, to garnish, if desired

Heat oil or butter in a heavy-bottomed frying pan, add fish and cook gently for 4 to 5 minutes on each side, or until cooked

60

through. The time depends on the thickness of the fish, do not overcook or it will be dry and like cottonwool! Peel and grate apples into a serving bowl, pour over orange juice, then stir in sugar, vinegar, horseradish, cream, salt and pepper. Mix gently together and serve as an accompaniment to the fish.

For a dinner party, garnish the fish with slices of orange and sprigs of parsley.

Fried Fillets of Plaice or Sole with Orange

Try orange wedges instead of the more usual lemon to serve with fish fillets, which you have dipped in egg and breadcrumbs and fried.

Fried Liver with Orange

This favourite liver recipe comes from an old friend. Use fresh, not frozen, liver and leave it pink in the middle, so that it remains moist. Four ounces (125 g) liver is usually enough to allow per person.

Serves 4
1 lb (500 g) lamb's liver, in the piece
2 oz (60 g) plain flour
salt and freshly ground black pepper
2 teaspoons finely chopped fresh thyme or
1 teaspoon dried
2 teaspoons grated orange peel
2–3 oz (60–90 g) butter
6 fl oz (185 ml) orange juice
4 fl oz (125 ml) port

Wash and dry liver, then slice very, very thinly. On a large plate mix together flour, salt, pepper, thyme and orange peel, coat each liver slice on both sides with this mixture. To do this simply press liver into flour mixture

Minneola

first on one side then the other. (I find this method much better than shaking ingredients all together in a plastic bag.)

Heat 2 oz (60 g) of the butter in a large frying pan over a low heat, add liver a few pieces at a time and fry quickly on each side, 1½ to 2 minutes should be enough. Remove to a hot dish and keep warm. When all liver is cooked, pour in orange juice and port, add remaining butter and bring to the boil, scraping the bottom of the pan well. Boil for 1 minute, strain and pour round the liver. Serve at once.

Lamb Casserole

This recipe should really be made with mutton but as this is almost impossible to get, use lamb. Stewing lamb with all the fat trimmed off will do. Peeling small onions isn't much fun but try working with the onions submerged in water – it helps reduce the tears!

Serves 4

2 lb (1 kg) lamb (trimmed weight)

24 button onions

2 fl oz (60 ml) olive oil

1/2 teaspoon crushed coriander seeds

2 cloves garlic, chopped

2 oz (60 g) shelled walnuts, roughly chopped

juice of 1 lemon

salt and freshly ground black pepper

2 oranges

1 tablespoon fresh coriander leaves, chopped

Greek-style plain yogurt, to serve

Cut carefully trimmed meat into 1½ in (4 cm) cubes, peel onions and leave whole. Heat oil in a heavy-bottomed flameproof casserole, add spice and lamb and stir-fry over a gentle heat for 5 to 7 minutes, then add onions and garlic, cover and cook very slowly for 30 to 40 minutes. Add walnuts, lemon juice, salt and pepper and simmer, covered, for a further 20 to 30 minutes, or until meat is very tender.

At this stage the casserole may be cooled and refrigerated or frozen.

To finish, thaw if frozen and reheat. Peel oranges, trimming off all pith, chop into cubes, then add to casserole with coriander leaves, stir once or twice, then serve straightaway, accompanied by yogurt.

Orange, Pork & Mustard Casserole

Pork and orange complement each other beautifully and the grainy mustard adds extra bite to the dish.

Serves 5–6
1½ lb (750 g) pork
4 oranges
2 oz (60 g) butter
2 onions, chopped
1–2 tablespoons whole-grain mustard, or to taste
salt and pepper, to taste

Trim pork and cut into 1½ in (4 cm) cubes. Grate 2 teaspoons of orange peel from one of the oranges and squeeze the juice from two. Melt butter in a heavy-bottomed flameproof casserole, add onions and cook gently for 4 to 5 minutes. Add pork and stir-fry for 2 to 3 minutes, then add orange peel, orange juice, mustard, salt and pepper, stir once, cover and simmer gently over a low heat for ¾ to 1 hour, until meat is tender. Peel remaining 2 oranges, remove all pith, slice thickly, then chop roughly. Add to casserole and serve at once.

Orengis, almondis, and the pomegarnade, Lymons, datez.

(1430, Lydgate)

Chicken with Orange & Ginger

Serves 4

1 × 3½–4 lb (1.75–2 kg) roasting chicken, jointed

1 onion, sliced

1 orange, sliced

1½ teaspoons ground ginger

10 fl oz (315 ml) white wine

2 egg yolks

5 fl oz (155 ml) double (heavy) cream

salt and pepper, to taste

Remove skin and fat from chicken pieces. Place onion and orange in a roasting tin, sprinkle with ginger and pour over white wine. Next place a rack – a wire tray will do – in the pan and place chicken pieces on top. Cover tightly with foil. Place in a moderately hot oven, 190 °C (375 °F/Gas 5), and bake for 20 minutes, do not overcook.

Remove chicken pieces, wrap in foil and keep warm. Skim off any fat from pan juices, remove onion and orange and reduce liquid to 10 fl oz (315 ml). Beat egg yolks in a bowl and pour on boiling chicken juice. Return to pan and reheat. Stir in cream, salt and pepper and heat through, do not boil or sauce will curdle.

Transfer chicken to a serving dish and pour over sauce. Serve hot.

For fame, it is a squeezed orange; but for public good there is something to do.
(1822, George Canning the younger, 'George Canning (the elder) and his Times')

Orange Torte

This tart is especially good owing to the addition of Seville orange peel – made only with sweet orange, it is rather bland.

Serves 6
4 oz (125 g) butter
4 oz (125 g) sugar
4 eggs
2 oz (60 g) ground almonds
1 whole orange, minced, including skin
grated peel of 2 Seville oranges
2 teaspoons orange flower water
2 oz (60 g) plain flour
1 tablespoon biscuit or cake crumbs or semolina
cream, to serve

Cream butter and sugar together until light and fluffy, then add eggs one by one, beating well in between. Stir in almonds, minced orange, Seville orange peel and orange flower water. Lastly fold in flour. Butter an 8 in (20 cm) cake tin, dust with biscuit or cake crumbs or semolina and pour in orange and almond mixture.

Bake at 190 °C (375 °F/Gas 5) for 20 to 25 minutes, until rich golden-brown. Serve warm with thin or thick cream.

Note: if Seville oranges are unobtainable, ½–1 teaspoon grated grapefruit peel will sharpen the peel of 1 ordinary orange.

Dark Seville Orange Marmalade

This marmalade is nearly black and darkens with keeping. It is quite delicious.

Makes 3 lb (1.5 kg)
40 fl oz (1.25 litres) water
1 lb (500 g) Seville oranges
2 lb (1 kg) dark Barbados sugar
juice of 1 lemon

Place water and whole oranges in a large pan and simmer together for ¾ to 1 hour, or until fruit is easy to pierce with a knitting needle. Leave to cool, overnight if liked. When cold, remove fruit with a slotted spoon, reserving water, and chop fruit into small, chunky

Seville

pieces, removing all pips and coarse pieces as you work. Reserve pips and tie in a muslin bag.

Put fruit into a clean pan, add reserved water and bring slowly to the boil. Add sugar, stirring continuously, then add lemon juice and the bag of pips, tied with string to the handle of the saucepan. Continue stirring until sugar is dissolved, then increase the heat and boil fast until setting point is reached, see page 88. Remove from the heat, cool slightly, remove bag of pips and pot, see page 88. Store in a cool, dark cupboard.

Note: it is harder to reach a 'set' with Barbados sugar than with white sugar but it makes a tastier marmalade even if you don't achieve such a firm set.

Orange Mincemeat

This is a suetless mincemeat, light and fresh-tasting. It will keep in screw-topped jars in the bottom of the fridge for up to 6 weeks. To keep longer, store in the freezer.

grated peel and juice of 2 oranges
8 oz (250 g) Candied Orange Peel, see page 48
8 oz (250 g) glacé cherries
4 oz (125 g) almonds, blanched and roughly chopped
1 lb (500 g) currants
2 lb (1 kg) apples, peeled and cored
8 oz (250 g) dark brown sugar
2 teaspoons cinnamon
4 fl oz (125 ml) brandy, rum or whisky
8 oz (250 g) butter, very cold, to be added last

Grate orange peel into a large mixing bowl and strain in the juice, then add all other ingredients except butter. Mix well together. Take the cold butter and either grate it quickly into the mixture or chop it very finely and add. Mix well, then pot in sterile jars, cover and store in fridge or freezer.

The iuyce of orenges or lymons may be taken after meales in a lyttell quantitie.

(1539, Sir Thomas Elyot 'The castel of helth')

Orange Chutney
Makes 2½–3 lb (1.25–1.5 kg)
4 oranges
10–15 fl oz (315–470 ml) water
10 fl oz (315 ml) wine vinegar
2 lb (1 kg) brown sugar
1 teaspoon coriander seeds
2 cloves
2 in (5 cm) cinnamon stick
1 dried chilli pepper
4 oz (125 g) preserved ginger, chopped

Wipe oranges and cut into thick slices. Place in a saucepan and just cover with water. Cover and simmer until tender, 30 to 45 minutes. Cool, then remove oranges with a slotted spoon and cut into chunks. Return to a larger saucepan with the juices, add vinegar and sugar and heat gently until sugar is dissolved, stirring all the time. Tie spices into a piece of muslin, add to pan and cook gently for ¾ to 1 hour. Fifteen minutes before end of cooking time, add ginger. When cooked, cool slightly, remove spice bag and pour into clean, sterile jars, see page 88, cover and store on a cool, dry shelf.

73

Whole Clementine Preserve

This is useful to add to puddings and creams or to chop up and serve with ice cream. The fruit can also be used in place of candied peel. It makes a very pretty gift.

30 fl oz (940 ml) water
1 lb (500 g) sugar
12 clementines
1–2 tablespoons brandy, rum or whisky,
if desired

Heat water and sugar together in a large, shallow saucepan over a low heat until dissolved. Prick clementines all over with a darning needle. When sugar is dissolved, add fruit, cover and simmer slowly for ¾ to 1 hour or until fruit begins to look translucent. Cool slightly, then pack fruit into wide-necked jars and top up with syrup. A little brandy may be poured over the fruit before topping up with syrup. Cover and store in a cool, dry place.

Keep for at least 6 weeks before using if you have added brandy or other alcohol, such as rum or whisky.

Tangerine Jelly

A superb jelly, quite unlike anything out of a packet.

Serves 4
½ oz (15 g) powdered gelatine
4 fl oz (125 ml) water
12 fl oz (375 ml) tangerine juice, see page 19
1–2 oz (30–60 g) caster sugar, or to taste

TO FINISH
3–4 fresh tangerines
2 fl oz (60 ml) brandy

Mix gelatine and water together in a small saucepan and place over a low heat. Add tangerine juice and sugar and heat gently until gelatine is dissolved, stirring all the time, do not allow to boil. Pour into a 1 pint (0.75 litre) mould and leave to set.

Peel tangerines, remove all pith, pips and white, stringy bits, place in a bowl, toss with brandy and leave to marinate for 30 minutes or longer, if liked. To serve, dip mould in hot water and turn out. Place marinated tangerine segments round the jelly.

Clementine Mallow

A light fluffy dessert – good after a rich dinner.

Serves 6–8
7 clementines
30 marshmallows
2 teaspoons powdered gelatine
2 tablespoons water
2 egg whites
2–3 fl oz (60–90 ml) Cointreau

Grate peel of 1 clementine and squeeze juice into a small, heavy-bottomed saucepan. Cut marshmallows in half and add to juice and peel. Slowly dissolve over a very low heat, taking care they do not burn: do not allow to boil. When dissolved, remove from heat and leave to cool. Heat gelatine and water together in a small saucepan over a low heat until dissolved, then leave to cool slightly.

Peel remaining clementines, divide into segments, remove all pith, pips and stringy white bits and reserve. Stir gelatine into mallows. Whip egg whites in a bowl until stiff and carefully fold in mallow mixture, then fold in clementine segments. Pour into a pretty glass serving dish and leave to set. Before serving, pour over the liqueur.

GRAPEFRUIT

These large, juicy fruit have a sweet-sharp, refreshing taste. They are all too often used only as a breakfast food or as a rather dull cold starter. However, they are excellent in salads, with some vegetables and with fatty, rich meats, such as duck and pork. It is worth noting, though, that as grapefruit has a strong and distinctive flavour, it is best, if you are using it in a main course dish, to avoid serving a fine wine with this course.

Hot Grapefruit & Carrots

Carrots have a sweetness not always enjoyable in a vegetable but grapefruit, with its marvellous tart flesh, goes superbly with them. Serve this dish with pork or duck, or perhaps with goose at Christmas time.

Serves 6
2 grapefruit
1½ lb (750 g) carrots
salt and freshly ground black pepper
2 oz (60 g) butter
½ teaspoon crushed coriander seeds
2 teaspoons sugar
2 tablespoons chopped fresh parsley

Using a sharp knife, peel grapefruit, remove all pith and cut out the segments. Set aside. Scrape carrots and cut into quarters, sixths or eighths lengthwise, depending on how thick they are. If carrots are very long, halve them. Cook in salted water (or steam) until just beginning to be tender. Drain. Heat butter in a large frying pan, add carrots, coriander seeds, sugar, extra salt if necessary and pepper. Stir-fry together for 3 to 4 minutes, add grapefruit, heat through, sprinkle with parsley and serve.

Duck with Grapefruit

A pleasant change from the more usual duck
with orange.

1 duck
3 grapefruit
1 onion, quartered
6–8 fresh sage leaves
6 fl oz (185 ml) port
salt and pepper, to taste
1–2 teaspoons sugar

Wipe inside duck, clean and trim off all ex-
cess fat inside and at both openings. Cut one

grapefruit into chunks, peel and all, mix with onion and sage leaves and stuff the duck cavity. Grate peel from second grapefruit and reserve. Squeeze the juice and pour over the duck. Sprinkle the breast with the grated peel. Cover the breast with foil and roast for 1½ hours at 180°C (350°F/Gas 4). Baste frequently during the cooking and remove foil 10 to 15 minutes before end of cooking time to allow the skin to brown. Transfer to a hot serving dish and keep warm while making the gravy.

Squeeze juice from remaining grapefruit. Skim all fat from meat juices in pan, pour in grapefruit juice and bring to the boil, boil rapidly for 1 to 2 minutes, scraping the bottom of the meat pan thoroughly. Add port, salt, pepper and sugar, bring to the boil and strain into a warm sauceboat to serve with the duck.

Spiced Pork Patties with Grapefruit

These mild, curry-flavoured pork patties can be made with fresh pork mince or minced left-over meat from a pork joint. Make sure it is well cooked.

Serves 4–5
1 lb (500 g) pork mince
1 oz (30 g) breadcrumbs
1 teaspoon mild curry powder
salt and pepper, to taste
1 egg, beaten
1 tablespoon milk, if needed
2 grapefruit
3–4 spring onions, green and white parts
finely chopped
2–4 sage leaves, chopped
2 oz (60 g) butter
2 fl oz (60 ml) cooking oil

Combine pork, breadcrumbs, curry powder, salt and pepper in a mixing bowl. Mix together well, then add beaten egg and press mixture into a ball. If mixture seems too dry, add milk. Make into small cakes, patties or sausage shapes. Set aside while preparing grapefruit accompaniment.

Peel grapefruit, remove all pith and stringy bits and cut out the segments, reserving all the juice. Squeeze out the left-over grapefruit core to extract all remaining juice.

Melt butter in a saucepan, add spring onions, sage leaves, grapefruit juice and segments and cook gently with a little salt and plenty of pepper for 3 to 4 minutes.

To cook the patties, heat oil in a frying pan, add patties a few at a time and cook for 4 to 5 minutes on each side, or until cooked through. Keep warm on a hot platter in the oven as you cook the others. Serve with the hot grapefruit relish.

A Hot Grapefruit Dessert

One grapefruit will serve two people. To prepare the grapefruit, use a sharp knife and peel carefully, then remove all pith and stringy bits and cut out the segments. Reserve all juice and squeeze the core of the grapefruit to extract all remaining juice. Arrange the segments in a flameproof serving dish and chill.

Melt 1½ oz (40 g) butter in a heavy-bottomed pan over a gentle heat, add 4 oz (125 g) soft brown sugar, 1 teaspoon garam masala (available from specialist grocers and delicatessens) and the juice from the grapefruit. Cook until the sugar has melted and the sauce is syrupy. Pour the hot, bubbling sauce over the grapefruit segments and serve at once.

The grapefruit segments and the sauce can be made in advance and chilled separately. Reheat the sauce before serving.

Grape-fruit. It looks and tastes much like a Shaddock, it does not bear the slightest resemblance to a grape.

(1885, Lady Brassey 'The Trades')

Grapefruit & China Tea
Sorbet

The smoky taste of China tea in this sorbet gives it a wonderful and elusive flavour. It can be served as a pudding, as an in-between course at a special dinner party or as a summer starter with avocados or kiwi fruits.

Serves 4–6
2 grapefruit
6 oz (185 g) sugar
20 fl oz (625 ml) water
2 teaspoons Lapsang Souchong tea or other smoked tea

TO FINISH
2 egg whites
2 oz (60 g) caster sugar

Grate a little grapefruit peel very carefully, taking extra care that no white pith gets included. Squeeze juice from both fruit and

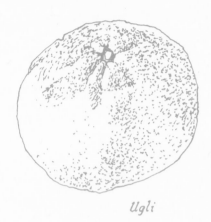

Ugli

reserve. Place grapefruit peel, sugar and water in a heavy-bottomed saucepan and bring to the boil. Boil for 3 to 4 minutes, add tea leaves, remove from the heat, stir well and leave to cool. When cold, add grapefruit juice and strain the mixture into a freezing container and freeze. When the mixture begins to turn to crystals, mix well and return to freezer for a further 30 to 45 minutes.

To finish, beat egg whites in a bowl until stiff, then gradually beat in caster sugar. Remove grapefruit mixture from freezer, stir well but do not allow to melt too much, then fold in egg whites carefully but thoroughly. Return to the freezer and freeze until firm.

BASICS

To Test Jam for Set

Remove saucepan or preserving pan from heat and put a little jam or jelly on to a cold plate. Leave to cool, then tilt the plate slightly. The jam is setting if it begins to wrinkle at this point.

If using a sugar thermometer, 'set' is reached at 110 °C/220 °F.

To Pot Jam, Curd or Preserves

Potting must be done correctly to keep food from developing bacteria.

Make sure that the jars are completely sterile, warm and dry. Remove any foam that may have formed on the surface of the jam and pot carefully and quickly. Fill jars to the brim, cover with wax circles, then seal with self-sealing lids. Label and store in a cool, dark place or the fridge, as directed.

Freezing Citrus Fruit

The joys and benefits of citrus fruit come from using them fresh; once frozen a percentage of their vitamin C content is lost and the wonderful oil in the skins no longer has that sharp, fresh tang. In spite of this, these fruits freeze quite well.

Seville oranges, wrapped in plastic bags and sealed, can be frozen whole as they are. Sweet oranges can be peeled and frozen whole. Alternatively, divide into segments and layer in plastic freezer boxes with sugar, using 6–8 oz (185–250 g) sugar to 1 lb (500 g) fruit segments. Cover and freeze. Grapefruit, tangerines, mandarins and clementines can all be treated in the same way. Kumquats can be frozen whole and added to pork and beef stews as a flavouring.

Lemons can be frozen whole, in slices or as juice. The peel may also be grated, tightly wrapped in plastic and frozen. Use this to add to stocks and sauces.

The juice of oranges, grapefruit and lemon, although it loses some of its vitamin C content, will freeze well for up to 4 months.

It is rather rough on the boy to suddenly discover that his father had sucked the orange, and that he has merely inherited the skin.
(1884, Hawley Smart 'From Post to Finish')

INDEX